ESCAPING THE PREDATORS

HOW ANIMALS USE CAMOUFLAGE

Animal Book for 8 Year Olds
Children's Animal Books

BABY PROFESSOR

EDUCATION KIDS

Speedy Publishing LLC

40 E. Main St. #1156

Newark, DE 19711

www.speedypublishing.com

Copyright 2017

In the animal world, if you aren't strong you had better be fast. But what do you do if you aren't the strongest or the fastest? You may need to be the most invisible!

Read on and learn how animals use camouflage to keep from being somebody's lunch.

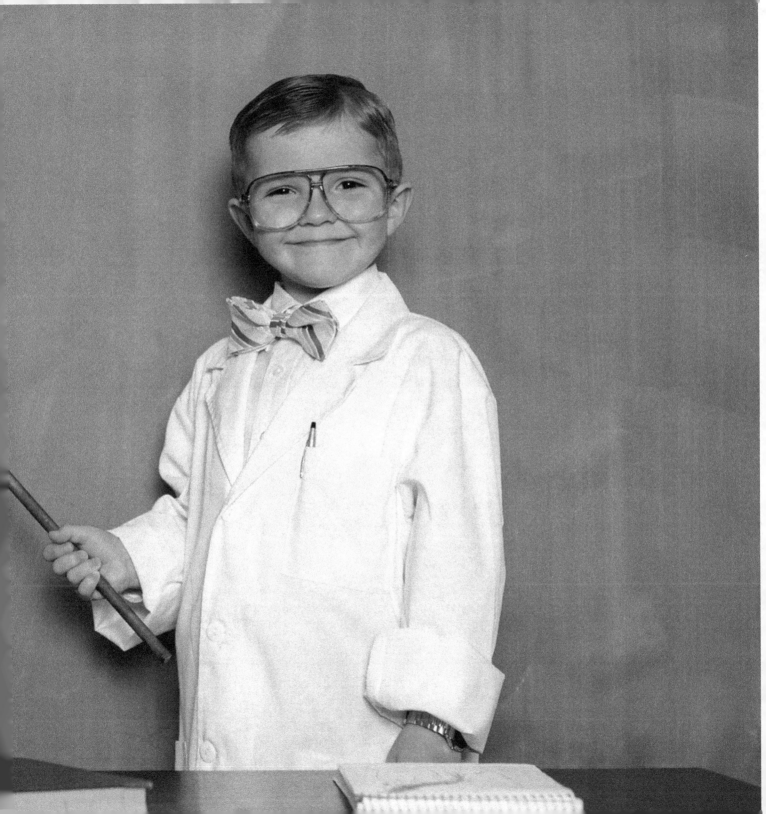

Southern Bell Frog

HIDING IN PLAIN SIGHT

. . . .

Hunters and soldiers can put on special clothing so they can blend into the scenery. Animals don't have that luxury: they have to figure out how to hide from those who want to eat them, using just their body's tools and talents.

There are three basic ways animals camouflage themselves: cripsis, mimesis, and motion dazzle. Let's look at each option.

CRIPSIS

. . . .

Cripsis is the art of looking like you aren't there. For animals who look for their prey mainly by sight, rather than by smell or sound, cripsis can be a strong defence.

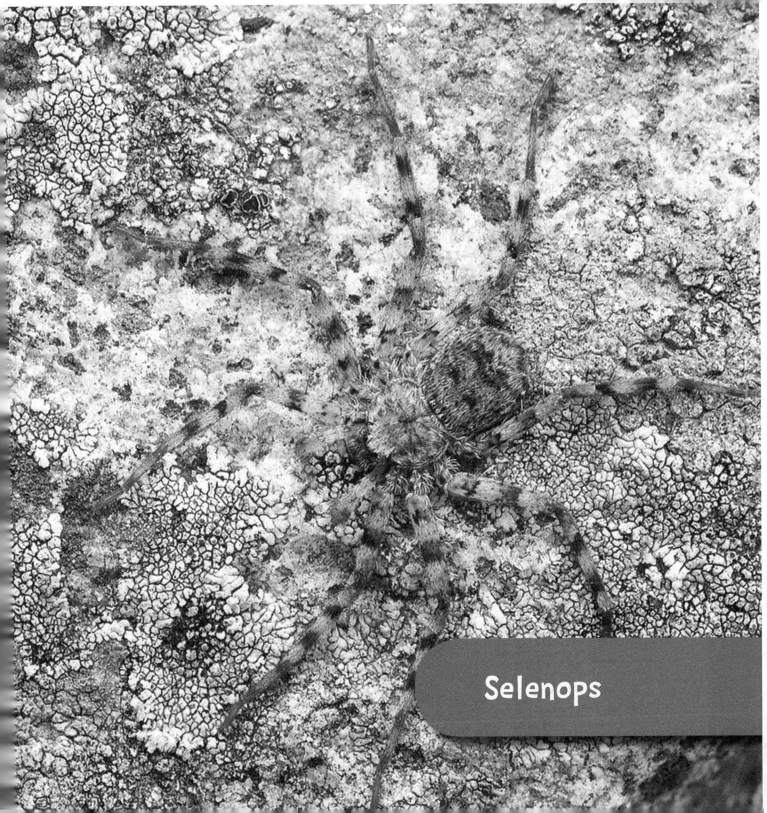

Selenops

Here are a number of ways you can practice cripsis.

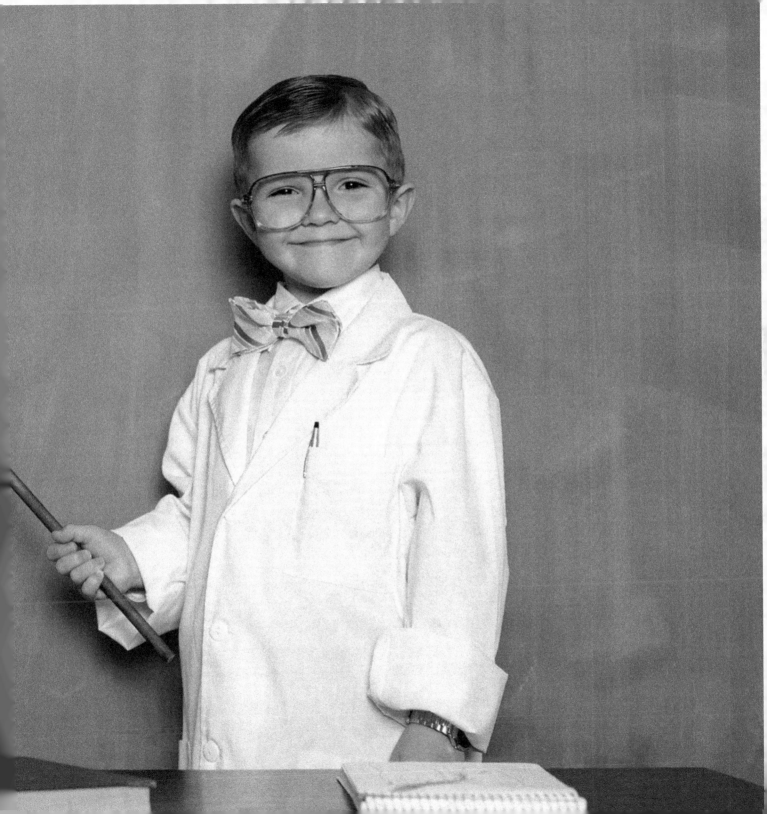

Camouflaged wild desert horned lizard

Blending into the background

If you stand in front of a blue wall, and you are blue yourself, it is harder for me to see you. Many animals try to blend with their background, even adjusting as needed. For instance, the Arctic fox wears white fur in the winter to blend with the snowy landscape, and gray-brown fur in the summer to better match the scenery.

Parakeets who live among the leaves of trees are generally green, while woodcocks are a speckled brown to match the forest floor where they live.

Desert dwellers, whether birds, mammals like foxes and gerbils, or lizards, tend to wear browns, ochres, and reddish hues to match the desert landscape.

Sphinx Moth

Camouflage

Scientists studied a particular species of moth in part of England between 1840 and 1950. The moths' colors matched well the bark of the trees they liked to live on. As that area of England developed more industry, increasing air pollution caused the trees' bark to get darker. The study noted that the moths' colors got darker to match the changing color of the trees.

This doesn't mean that animals consciously choose their colors to match their background. It is more likely determined by natural selection: the more visible members of a species are more likely to get eaten before they have children of their own, and so are less likely to pass on their genes for colorful fur or feathers.

Butterfly Camouflage

Leopards

Disruption

Disruptive patterns and colors break up the animal's outline, so it is harder for the hunting animal to figure out how big the intended prey is, or even where he starts. Predators like leopards also use disruptive patterns. Their spots look like the shadow pattern of leaves on the ground to other animals—sometimes until it is too late.

Giraffes have a disruptive pattern on their hides which is very useful for young giraffes, but less useful for adults. Young giraffes spend a lot of time lying down in the long grass to hide from predators while their parents are away feeding, and their irregular coloration helps them blend into the grasses if they stay very still. When giraffes are grown, they are less likely to stay still when a predator is near, and as soon as they move it becomes obvious where they are. Adult giraffes rely on their size and running ability to deal with most threats from animals right up to lions, rather than their ability to hold still among the trees.

Giraffes

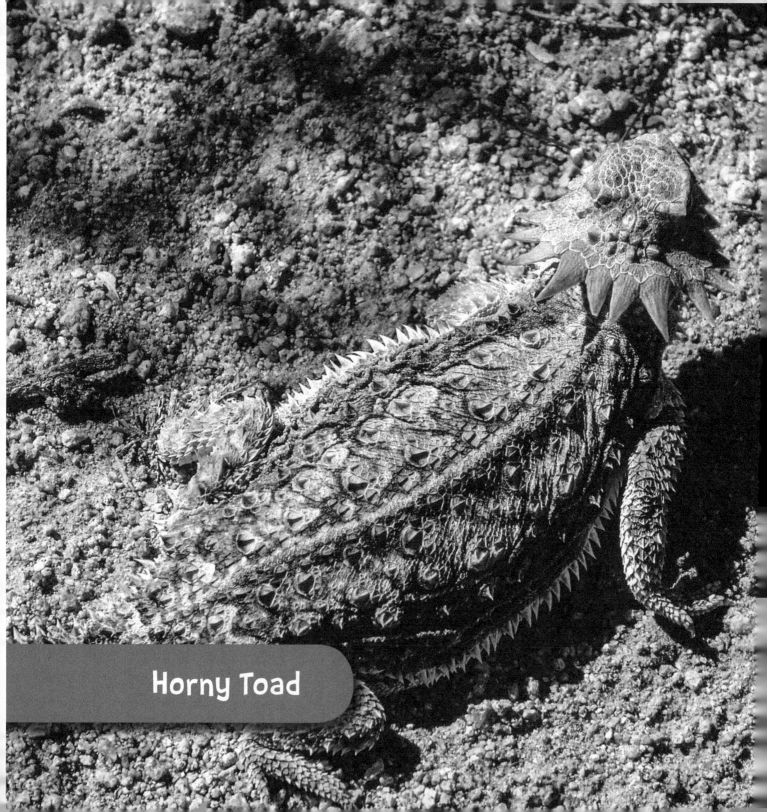

Horny Toad

Eliminating shadows

One way creatures conceal that they are there is by concealing their outline. If they can eliminate the shadow along the edge of their body or limbs, it will be harder for other creatures to see them. Creatures who use this method have flattish bodies that get thinner along the edge, and may have an irregular, frilled edge, like the horned lizards of North American deserts. The European nightjar, and other birds that rest on the ground, may turn to face the sun so that they cast a narrow, ambiguous shadow behind them. If they sat sideways to the sun, a hawk overhead would see clearly from their shadow what kind of tasty treat was sitting on the ground below them.

Self-decoration

Some creatures use parts of their environment to change their shape, color, or pattern. A decorator crab, for instance, covers its back with stones and seaweed. The blotched emerald moth uses little hooks on its body to attach leaf fragments to itself so each moth of the species has a quite different outline than all of its relatives.

Emerald Moth

Eastern Kingsnake

Cryptic behavior

If something with sharp eyes is hunting you, often the worst thing you can do is move or try to run away. Holding very still so you look like part of the landscape may save you.

Of course, if your background is moving, you had better move, too. The leafy sea dragon hides itself among seaweed, which it resembles. But it also makes sure to sway back and forth the way the seaweed is pushed by the motion of the water. If it stayed still, it would be pretty noticeable!

Leafy sea dragon among the seaweed

Leopard

Motion camouflage

This is an odd one that some animals use, sometimes to get close to possible mates and sometimes to get close enough to attack rivals. The animal moves slowly in a straight line toward the target: ideally, from the target's point of view the animals doesn't seem to be moving so much as getting slowly larger.

By the time the target figures things out, it may be too late to get away. To succeed, motion camouflage depends on the target you want to approach staying still so it cannot judge your motion against your background.

Leopard approaching

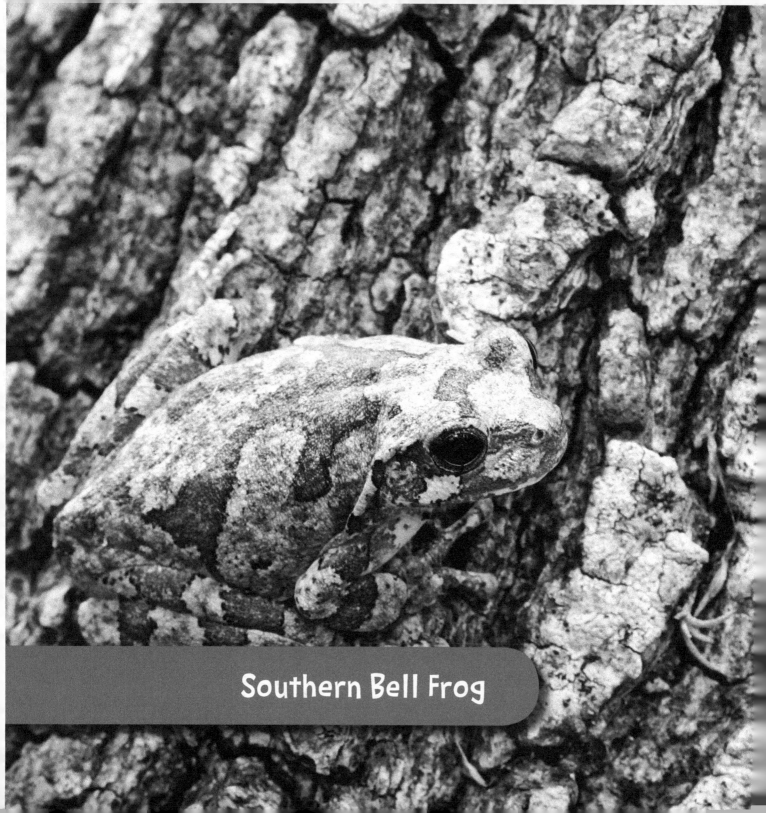

Southern Bell Frog

Changing skin pattern and color

It's not just chameleons who can change the color and pattern of their skin to help them hide better. Certain frogs, and fish like the peacock flounder, use these tricks. An octopus can not only change body color to blend into the background; it can change color to send signals to friends, mates, and rivals.

Special skin cells called chromatophores make the color change possible. Each chromatophore has pigment of one color only. In some animals, melanophore cells let the animal also adjust how dark its skin is.

Wide-eyed flounder

Tree Frog

Counter-shading

Normally, under the sun, an animal will appear lighter on the top, where the sun's rays strike, and darker in the lower part of its body. Many animals are lighter below and darker above to balance the sun-and-shade effect. The result is a flattening of the animal's coloration which lets it blend in more easily with a natural background.

There's another way animals use counter-shading. Some animals, like sharks, are light on the bottom and darker on top so they blend better against the lighter sky above them and the darker water below. The effect doesn't hide them from fish that are at the same level as the shark, of course, but the sharks do pretty well for themselves anyhow.

Reef Shark

Polpo comune

Counter-illumination

Some animals like squids have light-producing photophores all over their bodies. They can fire off sparkles of light so that their dark bodies show up less against a light background. It also confuses the shape a potential predator sees.

Transparency

Some creatures, like jellyfish, are almost transparent. This lowers their chances of being seen by prey, but the thinness of their muscles to permit the effect means that they cannot move very fast. Once they are found, they are likely to be dinner.

Jelly fish

Glass Catfish

Some Amazon River fish can at will make themselves almost entirely transparent. Some say this is just another case of the animal trying to match the background, since water is mostly transparent.

Silvering

Fish like sardines and herring are not transparent, but they are so highly reflective that it is harder for predators to pick them out from the glints and highlights in the water.

Sardines

Eyed Hawk-Moth caterpillar

MIMESIS

....

Mimesis, the second major camouflage method, is a way of looking like something you are not. An animal may do this to make itself look less interesting to someone who might otherwise want to eat it, or to put at ease some creature it wants to eat. Some caterpillars and other insects pretend to be twigs or leaves to appear less tasty.

Peacocks practice a form of mimesis with the huge "eye" patterns in their tail feathers. When they do a full feather display, the approaching predator may be scared off by the huge face that seems to be staring at him.

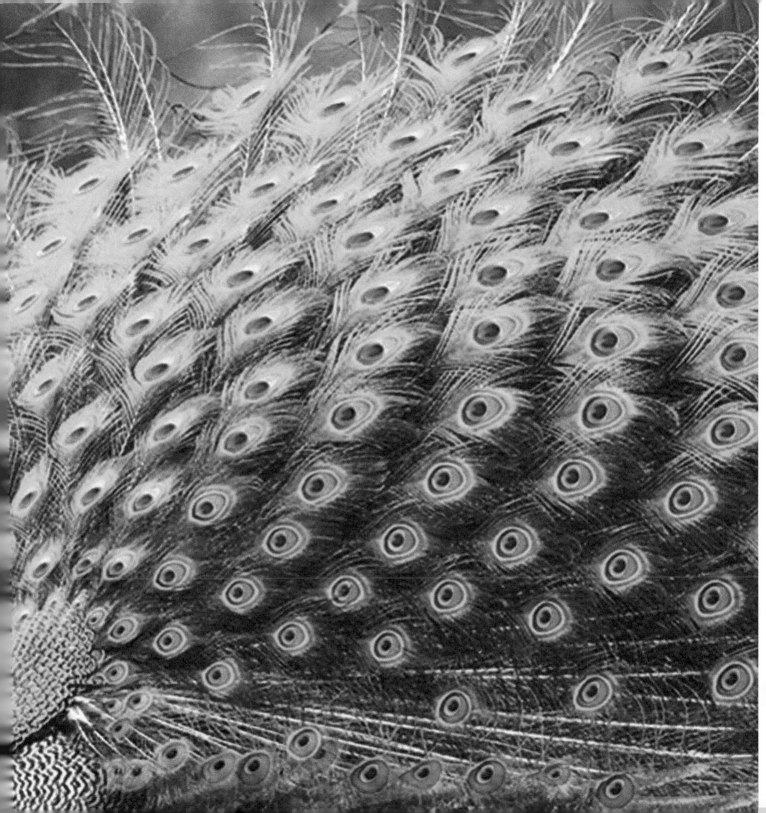

Pygmy sea horse

MOTION DAZZLE

· ·

Most of the time, camouflage only works if you stay still in relation to your background: the baby giraffe lies concealed among the grasses, hardly moving, while the seahorse makes itself sway to the rhythm of the seaweed it is attached to.

However, motion dazzle seeks to confuse your attacker while you are on the move. Bright, contrasting stripes of color that do not match the contours of the body make it harder for the attacker to be sure how fast the prey is moving or even how big it is. The zebra's pattern confuses lions when it is moving, and biting insects when it is standing still!

Zebras

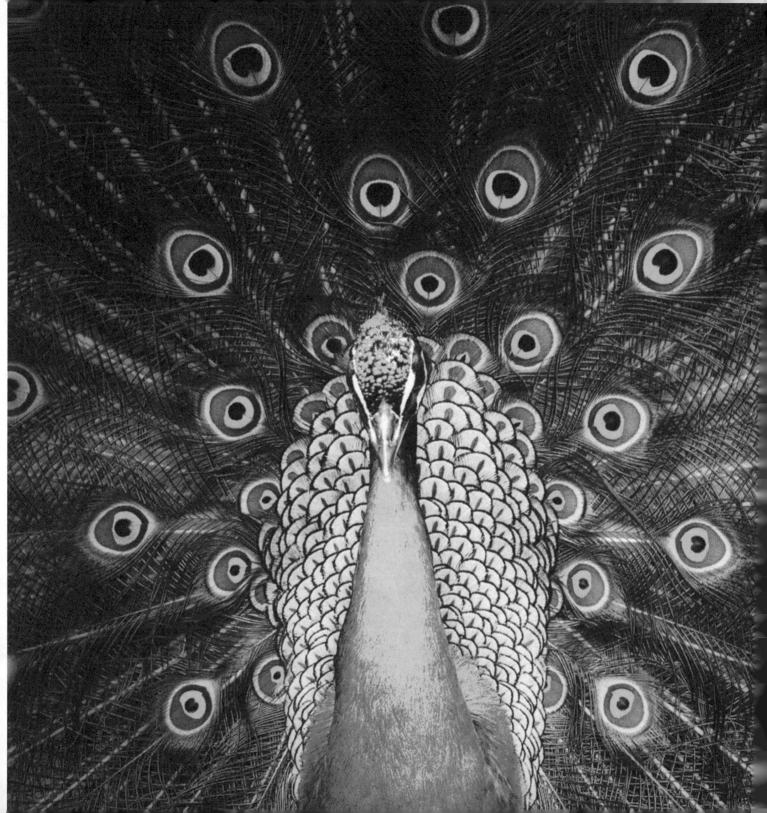

A WONDERFUL WORLD

· ·

Our world is full of wonders. Other Baby Professor books can help you learn about animals and plants of all kinds, from all around the world.

CPSIA information can be obtained
at www.ICGtesting.com
Printed in the USA
LVHW061253121219
640263LV00013B/203/P